junk foodie

51 DELICIOUS RECIPES FOR THE **LOWBROW GOURMAND**

written & photographed by *emilie baltz*

junk foodie

69¢
0 TRANS FAT

for m.p.

tous en moderation

Published by
Adams Media, a division of F+W Media, Inc.
57 Littlefield Street, Avon, MA 02322. U.S.A.
www.adamsmedia.com

ISBN-10: 1-4405-0641-8
ISBN-13: 978-1-4405-0641-3
eISBN 10: 1-4405-1089-X
eISBN 13: 978-1-4405-1089-2

Printed in China
10 9 8 7 6 5 4 3 2

Library of Congress Cataloging-in-Publication Data
is available from the publisher.

This book is available at quantity discounts for bulk purchases.
For information, please call 1-800-289-0963.

contents

acknowledgments

This book could not have been made tasty without the support and guidance
of a few select individuals: Wendy Simard, who thought this idea had more
to it than just junk; Mimi, Julia, Arthur, and all the people who have lived
with the crates of shelf stable food for months; Kate, who encouraged my
bad habits; Rinat and Johan, who taught me true dedication and drive; Allan
and Core 77, who first published this wacky idea; Tim, the brother who
will forever be the king of overeating crap; Marie Pierre and Joe, for never
allowing me to eat this stuff and making sure I grew up healthy, creative,
and independent; William Clark for the nuts n' bolts; Lydia and Meade for
introducing me to a thing called "pop"; Pierre and Lucie, for introducing me
to a thing called "la grande cuisine"; and Jason, for everything in between.

Bon appetit!

introduction

" I grew up in a house without junk food. My mother was French, and preached of everything in moderation. Each meal was incredibly creative, but, above all, healthy. We were humans, and that's what humans ate. Good, healthy food. Snack time at our house meant fruit wedges, toast, and maybe some juice. Maybe. The sugar-iest thing my brother and I had was the occasional box of Cinnamon Toast Crunch. And if my mom was away from the breakfast table, we'd eat three bowls as fast as we could, and then drink the milk. The last few gulps were so thick with cinnamon and sugar it felt like drinking delicious, edible, wet sand. Junk food, to me, was what aliens ate. And I was jealous of them. They lived all over town, in houses that looked and smelled different. They had cable TV, didn't need to clean their rooms, and some of them were even allowed to say the forbidden words, "Shut up!" In short, they were to be admired.

To balance this land of heathens, we'd fly off to France in the summer and eat things like Fois Gras and Tarte Amandine. The natives there said words like "merci!" and "s'il vous plait." It was a far cry from the land of Cinnamon Toast Crunch—in this world we used silver forks and knives, and supported the importance of apperitifs and elbows-off-the-table. Never, ever, would you dare ask for a thing called ketchup.

That was then. This is now. Today the French eat Twinkies and the Americans eat Fois Gras. It's somewhere in between that Junk Foodie evolved. Some call it fusion, I call it revolution. 'Cuz one rainy New York day, I sat at my desk dreaming up ways of making tasty distractions from the office snacks around me. And soon enough, an entire regime crystallized. And soon enough I left my job to make this stuff: Gross, delicious, ugly, beautiful, it was both alien and familiar. It was Junk Foodie.

I make no pretense of this being any good for you at all, but I do guarantee to delight, inspire, and make everyone giggle. Take it with a grain of . . . sugar(?) and practice moderation. Because too much of anything is no good at all. But not enough fun is a crime. Dig in! "

...Emilie Baltz, 2010

equipment & techniques

What it takes to be a Junk Foodie ···

junk foodie pantry EVERYTHING YOU NEED TO BE A JUNK FOODIE

LIQUIDS

Yoo-hoo

This sweet chocolate drink dates from the 1920s and is a great addition to any cocktail beverage or recipe that calls for a liquidy brown goo.

Kool-Aid

Nebraska's "official soft drink," this powder was created by inventor Edwin Perkins and his wife Kitty in 1927 to reduce the cost of shipping liquids.

Fanta

Inspired by German imagination ("Fantasie") after the Allies placed a trading ban on Nazi Germany during World War II, Fanta was a creative solution to quenching thirst using only ingredients available in Germany.

Nescafé

It took seven years to develop Nescafé for its release in Switzerland on April 1, 1938. Guess it takes about that amount of time to figure out "just add water."

Kool-Aid Fun Fizz

Soft Drink 2.0. Fun Fizz lets you have your Kool Aid—and fizzy too. Drop it in any Junk Foodie liquid for extra zing.

THESE INGREDIENTS CAN BE INTERCHANGED FOR ANY SIMILAR GENERIC
OR BRAND-NAME PRODUCT IN THE MARKETPLACE. THESE CHOICES DO NOT
REPRESENT ANY BRAND ALLEGIANCES. WE JUST THINK THEY TASTE GOOD.

LIQUIDS

These are some of
our faves. Mix 'em
up and enjoy!

Coca-Cola

Originally developed in
1886 as a nonalcoholic
version of French Wine
Coca, Coke was first
used medicinally to treat
diseases. See. it is good
for you.

Ginger Ale

This spicy stuff was the first
U.S. soft drink, originating
in 1866 and modeled after
imported Irish beers. Today
it's used for all sorts of
good stuff. Motion sickness
remedy included.

Root Beer

This root-based beverage
is made of more spices
than there are continental
states. Well, maybe not,
but it does have a ton of
flavor and is the beverage
that was first popularized
in the USA.

Nestea

It might not seem like
junk food, but given that the
sweetness of this bottled
beverage places it in the
same category as soft
drinks, we thought to add it
in for a drop of health.

7Up

Get this, 7Up was first sold
under the name "Bib-Label
Lithiated Lemon-Lime Soda,"
and was launched a couple
weeks before the Wall Street
Crash of 1929. It contained
mood-enhancing drugs and
claimed to cure hangovers.
Now there's a reason to get
"Up" in the morning.

Grape Soda

Hey. It's purple. 'Nuff said.

junk foodie pantry

From corn to potato, here's the stuff chips are made of.

Pork Rinds

OK. These might not be so great for your figure, but come on, you know you love 'em! Plus, you'll need some kind of meat-y product in your pantry. (Unless you're a pig. Then you shouldn't be reading this. Actually, you probably can't read this.)

Sour Cream and Onion Chips

Potato chips rule. You can use 'em for extra crunch, or in this case, a lil' creamy oniony kick that's sure to please.

Onion and Garlic Chips

Sure, these things'll give you bad breath to the max, but the garlicky, salty goodnes they lend to any dish will get you your friends back. We promise.

Potato Sticks

Chip-in-stick-form. Brilliant. Use 'em to get that gourmet julienne look 'n' feel for the best of your Junk Foodie recipes.

Sun Chips

We're all about balanced meals, so we had to throw in the Sun Chips. Yup. They're good for you. For sure. And there's a heart-shaped doodad on the package. So that's proof enough that you can eat seven packs and feel great, right?

Fritos

Hey! These are vegan! And the guy who started the company paid $100 for the original recipe! What an investment! Smash 'em up for some totally corny ingredients.

Barbecue-flavored Chips

No one really know where BBQ came from, but it is thought that "barbecue" may derive from the word "barabicu" which translates as "sacred fire pit." Proving once again that there's more than just spice 'n' rub in here.

Cheetos

These puffy guys are made of corn and water, then rolled in a variety of ingredients to flavor 'em. They're our favorite product to smash. The super-fine orange powdered stuff you're left with is awesome for coating. Not sniffing, though. Do not sniff it. Ever.

Salt 'n Vinegar Chips

For a bit of a twist, add in some of these sour crunchy bits to make your recipes that much more sassy.

Red Hot Chips

This is the stuff that stains your fingers red hot, so be careful when handling. No one likes a blushing pinkie finger.

junk foodie pantry

SALTY STUFF

Peanuts

There's really nothing better than a handful of super-salty roasted peanuts. Especially after swimming in a chlorinated pool. Give it a try. Unless you have a peanut allergy. Or a chlorine allergy. Then please refrain from either. Or both.

Cheese Crackers and Peanut Butter Crackers

From the makers of the Girl Scout Cookie comes the ultimate two-in-one Junk Foodie ingredient. Offering both cheese and peanut fillings, along with some buttery wheaty stuff, the pro Junk Foodie will love to deconstruct to get more bang for your buck.

Relish

Squeezable pickled cucumber. Sounds great, huh?

Mayo

Mayonnaise. Oh, you make the world go round. This emulsified goo helps everything taste just a lil' bit better. We encourage you to ask for extra packs next time you're at the deli. Then stash them in a drawer for your next Junk Foodie meal.

Ketchup

Did you know the largest ketchup packet weighed 1,500 pounds, and was 8x4 feet tall and 9½ inches wide?! These are much smaller. So get a lot of 'em. They're the life blood of the Junk Foodie.

Mustard

This is one ancient condiment. It dates back to Roman times when these old-school cooks mixed unfermented grape juice with mustard seeds. They liked it a bunch. So much that centuries later we're still using it. Think Julius Caesar would like the squishy pack?

Cheesy, spicy, gooey, and crunchy flavors here. Use these ingredients to give an extra spice to your Junk Foodie feast.

Nacho Cheese Doritos

Doritos means "little bits of gold" in Spanish. No wonder we like to hoard massive amounts of these crispy snacks in our pantry. Make sure to invest in a kilo. Ahem.

Cool Ranch Doritos

Think of these like all the chips combined. A medley of flavors, from sour cream and mayo, to green onlion and garlic, the Ranch Dorito has nuthin' to do with the cowboy ancestors of Americana, but it sure is a melting pot, chip-ified.

Handi-Snacks

The 1980s brought us Madonna and the Fresh Prince, but nothing as non-perishable as Handi-Snacks compartmentalized cheese n' crackers. Try the Premium varietal for a step up from those flat breadstuffs.

Cheez-Its

They're addictive. Seventeen packs disappeared during the making of this book. No cheese was harmed in the eating.

Popcorn

An American commodity, popped corn is our oldest, most authentic snack. What started as a gesture of friendship between natives and immigrants now covers movie theater floors. How's that for evolution?

Ramen

A true wonder of modern man. Ramen Instant Lunch cups can transform from dry to super soup in a matter of minutes.

junk foodie pantry

SWEET STUFF

The cream and filling of these tasty treats can be whipped and mashed to create a variety of pastry delights.

Chocolate Cupcake

The creamy center makes this one-cup portion of a sweet treat the stuff dreams are made of.

Ho Hos

Chocolate. Rolled. Delicious. The Ho Ho's got nothin' to do with Santa Claus, but sure does make for a merry treat. Check it out in the Ho Ho Buche de Noël recipe and you won't need anything else for Christmas.

Donettes

Two million of these bite-sized cake-in-a-ring-things are consumed every year. That's enough to cover lots of football fields.

Twinkies

The name of this cream-filled treat was inspired by a 1930s ad for Twinkle-Toe Shoes. Hmmm . . . still doesn't explain why they last forever.

Cracker Jacks

This is one old snack. It was first whipped up in 1893 by brothers Fritz and Louis for the first Chicago World's fair.

Pop-Tarts

Introduced in 1964, the Pop-Tart name was inspired by that king of retro art movements, "Pop Art." These toaster-ready breakfast treats were not only hip, but advanced. The packaging was adapted from a process normally used for dog food packing. Delicious.

SWEET STUFF

Little Debbie Strawberry Shortcake

A pinwheel of strawberry and cream, this Little Debbie snack is a whirly wind of wonder! Or cake. It might just also be cake.

Animal Crackers

Sure, kids love 'em, but come on, who can resist biting the head off a chimpanzee?

Little Debbie Banana Twins

Rare are the banana-flavored junk foods, so guard these like potatoes in 1840s Ireland.

Fruit Pies

Available in a variety of flavors and expiration dates, choose your pies wisely. Here are the flavors we suggest for well-balanced Junk Foodie meals: cherry, peach, pineapple, blueberry, and "All-American Apple."

junk foodie pantry

SWEET STUFF

Cookies, candies, sugar, and fluffiness.

Fluff

In the early twentieth century, a man named Archibald Query went door-to-door selling his sweet, spreadable marshmallow goo in Somerville, MA. Imagine that scene? The milkman, the ice man, the *marshmallow* man? Times have changed, but fluff stays just as addictive and delicious as ever. Thanks, Archie!

Fun Dip

Face it. This is just sugar. Sugar in a pouch with a sugar spoon. And it sure is delicious. Use it here for decorating, flavoring, and added energy buzz.

Whoppers

The ancestor of the original malted milk ball was called the Giant. Since 1949 they've been known as Whoppers. Neither brand should be confused with football teams or fast-food sandwiches.

Hershey's Kisses

One of the most popular American candies, these Kisses of chocolate most likely got their name from the sound the machine makes when dropping 'em out.

Starlight Mint Candies

You can buy these or just collect them from various diners around the country.

Mounds

We didn't really feel like a nut, so this pantry only holds the coconut/dark chocolate sibling of the famous candy bar duo. It's perfect for picking apart and adapting to a variety of far-out recipes.

Oreo

This is the best-selling cookie of the twentieth century. Strangely enough its name may come from the Greek root "orexin" (for appetizing) or "anorexic" (loss of appetite). The built-in paradox makes perfect sense for this black 'n' white, creamy 'n' crunchy delight.

Chocolate Chip Cookie

Classic junk food. You can't get much better than this. Go ahead, dip 'em in milk, pick all the chips out, throw them at your brother's head. Kidding. Please don't do that. Whatever your cookie pleasure, this fundamental snack is sure to take you far in the Junk Foodie world.

Vanilla Pudding

In the Middle Ages, cooks discovered how to bind eggs together to create creamy fillings. Today, with thickeners and stabilizers replace the yolks in this creamy junk food.

Butterfinger Mini

Coined from the slang term "Butterfinger," which means a clumsy person, this delicate flaky peanut/chocolate treat might just slip out of your fingers if you're not careful. We're suggesting the minis here so you can keep a tight hold on 'em.

Reese's Peanut Butter Cup

These peanut butter chocolate cups date from 1928 (originally, not presently; always check expiration dates). Invented by Harry Burnett Reese in the confines of his basement, Reese's today are a staple for any pantry. Make sure to share.

Snickers

The best-selling candy bar of all times, Snickers might supply more than a sugar rush. With nougat and peanuts, it's a great addition to a Junk Foodie pantry.

junk foodie pantry

SWEET STUFFF

We all scream for candy. Here's some of the most useful kinds out there. Oh yeah, and a cereal and fruity thing thrown in for good health.

Hot Tamales

Chewy, cinnamony spice is a great addition to a variety of exotic Junk Foodie recipes. Stock up and dig in!

Dots

These retro gumdrops come six to a pack—a perfect serving for fruity garnish or a colorful splash.

Tootsie Pops

We don't really care how many licks it takes to get to the center of these chocolate treat–filled confections. They're tasty enough to dip, lick, and crunch into any meal.

Twizzlers

Add a lil' sizzle to your day with these candyrific ropes of gummyness. We love 'em as straws for beverages, and they also chop up real nice for added strawberry chewiness.

Tootsie Rolls

The smaller sibling of the Tootsie Pop, the Tootsie Roll was invented as an alternative to traditional chocolate candy that melted all over the place.

Fruit Roll-Ups

The late '70s brought us these pectin-based wonders. Their stretchy texture makes 'em the lycra of haute Junk Foodie. They're perfect for shaping, wrapping, and transforming even the most basic junk food into flights of fancy.

Jelly Belly Jelly Beans

It's the bouillon cube of junk food. The Jelly Belly will save your tastebuds by offering a plethora of fruit (and funny) flavors that take your Junk Foodie feast to new heights.

Candy Buttons

Colored sugar dots glued onto paper. Not much more to this one.

Welch's Fruit Snacks

Ostensibly healthy, these fruit-based snacks are as sugar-filled as the neighboring confections on this page—they might send ya reelin' into Berries 'n' Cherries overload if you eat four packages.

Wonka Puckerooms

Sweet and sour, the zing of these jelly gummies is a must-have for any well-rounded palate.

Corn Pops Cereal

Puffy, sweet balls of corn. They float in milk, but we prefer to smash 'em up and use 'em as the glue for treats that need a little all-American stick.

MICROWAVE

For heating and melting

MEASURING SPOON

For gourmet precision

PAPER PLATES

For perfect plating, get the good stuff

PLASTIC SPORK

Double-duty mixing utensil

PLASTIC KNIFE

Keeps the slicing safe

MICROWAVE-SAFE BOWL

Brings it all together

techniques

the smash

··· **Make nothing out of something.** This technique is a simple way of pulverizing most any bagged junk food. Simply pierce a tiny hole in the top of the bag to let air escape. Take care to keep contents away from face and eyes, then enthusiastically smash the contents until little to no texture is felt inside the bag. You should be left with a fine powder that is happily incorporated into many Junk Foodie recipes—but should never be sniffed.

the reserve

··· **Frosting to filler, or** using the whole junk. Reserving is a method by which a trained Junk Foodie can create a variety of ingredient opportunities by carefully deconstructing the called-for junk food into its fundamental components. This is a way to maximize your junk and think about the whole food, not just the sticky sweet frosting. Be prepared to focus on minutiae and be warned: Carefully reserving a layer of coconut filler may be daunting. It's important to keep your sporks clean and your paper plates ready. And if that doesn't work, drink some Mountain Dew.

petit breakfasts

Kickstartin' sugar highs ···

fluffy grits with caramel crumble

INGREDIENTS

1 small bag Fritos
1 box Cracker Jacks
1 teaspoon Fluff

Pulverize Fritos to a fine powder. Smash Cracker Jacks in box. Be careful to keep these objects away from eyes when smashing. Combine 1 teaspoon of Fluff with enough Fritos powder to create a dense paste. Place in bowl. Microwave on high for 15 seconds. Top with a puff of Fluff and smashed Cracker Jacks. Serve while gooey warm.

pop-tart brunch strudel

INGREDIENTS

1 Apple Pie filling
1 Handi-Snacks Cheese Dip
1 Brown Sugar Cinnamon Pop-Tart crust

Cut top off Apple Pie. Scoop out filling and place to side. Smear Handi-Snacks Cheese Dip on one side of reserved Brown Sugar Cinnamon Pop-Tart crust (see Banana Brown Sugar Churro recipe). Top with apple pie filling. Cover with other half of Pop-Tart crust. Cut edges off to form a neat rectangle shape. Serve.

 +  +  =

triple berry compote parfait

1 Twinkie filling
1 Cherry Pie filling
1 package Berries 'n Cherries Fruit Snacks

Cut Twinkie in half and reserve cream. Put Twinkie cake aside for future use. (You can refrigerate the Twinkie cake or place it in an airtight container at room temperature. Shelf life is nearly eternal.) Carefully remove top from Cherry Pie. Scoop out filling. Combine Cherry filling with Twinkie cream, reserving a tiny bit for garnish. Place a layer of Berries 'n Cherries Fruit snack in bottom of a glass. Top with cream/filling mixture. Garnish with reserved Twinkie cream and a fruit snack.

INGREDIENTS **cheese scone**

1 pack Keebler Cheese and Crackers
1 serving Twinkie dough
1 small bag Cheetos

Remove Keebler Cheese and Crackers from wrapper and separate halves. Scoop cheese paste off crackers and put to side. Smash 2 crackers into a fine powder. Use reserved Twinkie cake dough from Triple Berry Compote Parfait recipe and knead it into a doughy ball. Fold in cracker powder and a splash of water to make a firm, gooey dough. Add reserved cheese paste. Knead all together until well incorporated. Form into scone shape. Microwave for 15 seconds. Smash Cheetos and scones and top with powder. Serve warm.

aztec coffee cake

1 Chips Ahoy! cookie
2 Oreo cookies
3 Hot Tamales

Smash Chips Ahoy! into crumbly mixture. Separate Oreos and reserve cream. Smash Oreo cookies into fine powder. Cut Hot Tamales into small chunks. Combine Oreo powder, half of Chips Ahoy! mixture, and Hot Tamale chunks. Add splash of water. Mix to fine paste. Place in small ramekin and microwave for 20 seconds. Remove and let cool. Demold. Top with Oreo cream and remaining Chips Ahoy! crumble. Add Hot Tamale garni for an extra sizzle.

 +  +  =

banana brown sugar churro

INGREDIENTS

1 package Banana Twins
3 Chips Ahoy cookies
1 Brown Sugar Cinnamon Toaster Strudel

Smash Banana Twins together to form a doughy mess. Keep kneading together until the dough firms. Roll into a long cylinder. Smash 3 Chips Ahoy! cookies to a fine powder. Remove all chocolate chips and reserve. Cut Brown Sugar Cinnamon Toaster Strudel in half. Scrape out filling. Microwave filling for 5 seconds or until more gooey and spreadable. Carefully spread over Banana Twin cylinder. Roll churro in Chips Ahoy! powder. Enjoy warm.

les lunches

Yup. You can have your cake and eat it (for lunch) too ....

 +  +  +  + =

waldorf salad tropicale

INGREDIENTS

1 Apple Pie filling
1 bag Salt 'n Vinegar Chips
4 Grape Puckerooms
6 Green Apple Jelly Bellies
1 packet mayonnaise

Remove top from Apple Pie. Remove filling for salad (reserve for another Junk Foodie creation). Smash a handful of Salt 'n Vinegar chips to a fine powder. Cut 4 grape-flavored Puckerooms into small chunks. Chop 6 Green Apple Jelly Bellies into bits. Mix all together. Stir in 1 packet of mayonnaise. Serve chilled.

INGREDIENTS   *welsh rarebit*

1 pack Keebler Cheese and Crackers Separate Keebler Cheese and Crackers and scrape off cheese filling.
2 packets mustard Mix cheese filling with 2 packets of mustard. Smear over crackers.
1 packet ketchup Top with dollop of ketchup. Microwave for 30 seconds or until bubbling.
Serve hot.

corn pop pancakes with satay dipping sauce

INGREDIENTS

1 pack Keebler Peanut Butter and Crackers
1 cup Corn Pops
1 packet mayonnaise
Snack Pack Vanilla Pudding
3 Hot Tamales

Separate Keebler Peanut Crackers and scrape off peanut butter filling. Reserve. Smash remaining crackers into a fine powder. Smash Corn Pops into a fine powder as well. Combine pulverized products with 1 packet of mayonnaise. Mix well until a dough results. Roll dough out into a thin layer. Cut into small circles. Simultaneously, for satay dipping sauce, mix reserved peanut butter filling with 1 tablespoon of Snack Pack Vanilla Pudding and a splash of water until well incorporated. Microwave pancakes for 1 minute. Top with a dollop of peanut paste and garnish with a Hot Tamale. Serve warm with dipping sauce.

jelly belly salteñas

INGREDIENTS

1 bag Cool Ranch Doritos
1 bag Red Hot Utz Chips
3 packets ketchup
Handful Jalapeño and Lime Jelly Bellies
1 Apple Pie top crust

Pulverize equal parts Ranch Doritos and Red Hot Utz Chips. Mix together with 3 packets of ketchup. Finely chop a few Jalapeño and Lime Jelly Bellies. Add to chip mixture, stirring well. Place Apple Pie shell bottom from Waldorf Salad recipe crust side down. Place chip mixture on one half of the top. Fold top over to create a half moon/empanada shape. Heat in microwave for 20 seconds. Serve with Jelly Belly garnish.

+

+

+

+

=

INGREDIENTS **french onion soup**

12 Utz Onion Rings
2 cups hot water
1 bag Cheetos

Place a dozen Utz Onion Rings in a bowl filled with 2 cups water. Microwave for one minute or until hot. Pulverize Cheetos and sprinkle over top of hot onion soup. Garnish with Onion Rings.

INGREDIENTS

tom khaa ramen

1 cup Instant Lunch Shrimp Ramen
1 small Mounds bar
Hot water
5 packets ketchup

Prepare ramen per package directions. Meanwhile, peel off outer chocolate layer of Mounds bar and reserve chocolate for use in Mocha Nougat Fondant recipe. Put ½ coconut filling to side. Combine remaining coconut filling with 1 teaspoon ketchup. Add 1 teaspoon hot water and stir until well combined. Add mixture to ramen when ready. Stir remaining 4 packets of ketchup into the ramen. Roll remaining coconut filling into a ball. Place on top of soup for decoration.

INGREDIENTS

cheddar relish ploughman

6 Cheez-Its
1 packet relish
3 Utz Onion Rings

On top of one Cheez-It cracker, place a small spoon of relish and top with crushed Utz Onion Ring. Layer with another Cheez-It to create a true workman's lunch. (Makes 3 sandwiches.)

crispy potato plantain torta

INGREDIENTS

1 package Banana Twins
2 packets mayonnaise
Handful potato sticks
1 small bag Salt 'n Vinegar potato chips
1 small bag Cool Ranch Doritos

Separate Banana Twins and remove all cream filling (reserve for another recipe). Top one side of the Banana Twin with a layer of mayonnaise. Top the other half with a layer of potato sticks. Close halves to form a sandwich. Smash Salt 'n Vinegar Chips and Cool Ranch Doritos together to yield a fine crumb coating. Cover sandwich with a thin layer of mayonnaise and roll in Dorito/chip coating. Serve with additional mayonnaise for dipping.

 +  +

 +  =

balinese spring roll suzette

INGREDIENTS

2 Orange Fruit Roll-Ups
A few potato sticks
1 Mounds bar coconut filling
Handful Utz Red Hot Chips
6 Pink Grapefruit Jelly Bellies

Unroll Fruit Roll-Up and tear off the Orange layer. Lay flat and place a neat row of potato sticks in center. Remove chocolate coating from Mounds bar. Smash Utz Red Hot Chips and combine with coconut filling until well incorporated. Form into small mounds and place on top of potato sticks layer. Cut Pink Grapefruit Jelly Bellies into small chunks and sprinkle over top of coconut mixture. Roll up Fruit Roll-Up into a neat bundle. Serve with chopsticks.

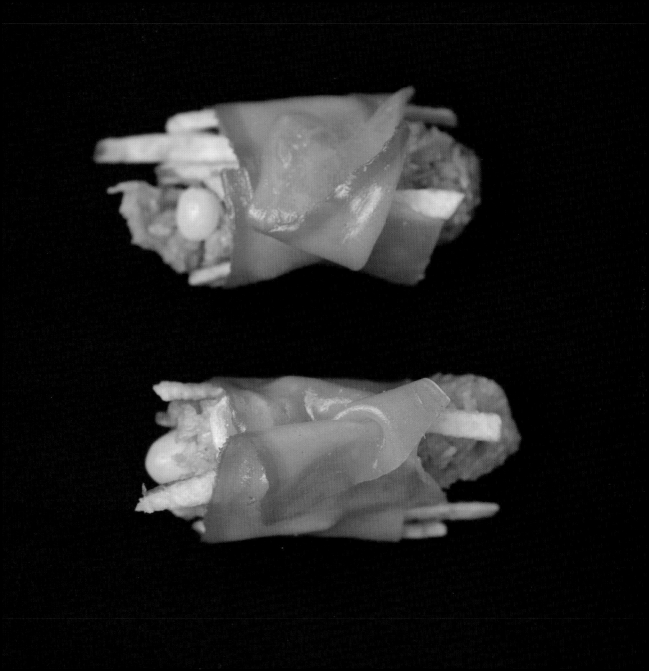

sweet 'n' salty tea sandwiches

INGREDIENTS

1 bag potato chips
6 animal crackers
2 packets mayonnaise

Smash 1 bag potato chips to fine crumbs. Set aside. Choose 3 pairs of matching, intact, unbroken animal crackers. Place flat side down and squirt a glob of mayonnaise on one face of each pair of crackers. Top with a pinch of smashed potato chip. Cover with matching chip. Bite off head first.

grands dinners

Decadence does come in a Dorito ....

INGREDIENTS

potato dauphinoise three ways

1 bag Utz Sour Cream and Onion Chips
1 bag Utz Salt 'n Vinegar Chips
1 serving potato sticks
1 pack Handi-Snack

Select several fully intact Sour Cream and Onion Chips. Pulverize a handful of Salt 'n Vinegar Chips. Layer whole Sour Cream and Onion Chip with several potato sticks. Top with Salt 'n Vinegar dust and a blob of Handi dip cheese. Repeat to create a layered form. Microwave for 15 seconds. Serve bubbly warm.

malaysian pork belly pot pie

INGREDIENTS

1 Pineapple Pie
1 pack pork rinds
1 bag Utz Red Hot Chips
3 Hot Tamales
3 Piña Colada Jelly Bellies
2 packets ketchup
1 pack peanuts

Remove top from Pineapple Ple. Remove filling and reserve. Smash Pork Rinds with force (note that Pork Rinds can be a bit tough, so we recommend using a mallet or other blunt implement of destruction). Pulverize Utz Red Hot Chips into chunks. Cut a few Hot Tamales into bite-sized pieces. Combine filling, pork rinds, Red Hot powder, Hot Tamale bits, Piña Colada Jelly Bellies, 2 packets ketchup, and 1 pack peanuts. Place mixture into empty Pineapple Pie crust. Re-cover with pie top. Heat in microwave for 30 seconds. Serve hot.

=

= + + +

homestyle mafé veggie burger

INGREDIENTS

1 pack peanuts
1 bag Nacho Cheese Doritos
1 bag Cheetos
3 packets ketchup
¼ cup water

Crush peanuts, Doritos, and Cheetos together. Add ketchup. Mix to form a paste. Add in water until mixture is moist, but not runny. Press mixture into bottom of a microwave-safe cup (mixture should fill roughly ¼ of the cup). Microwave on high for 2 minutes or until bubbling. Remove from microwave and let cool. Invert from cup onto plate. Serve with condiment of choice.

gnocchi à la parisienne

1 Handi-Snacks Breadsticks 'n Cheez
1 small bag potato chips
7 packets ketchup

Smash Handi-Snacks Breadsticks into a fine powder. Pulverize potato chips. Combine. Add ½ of Handi-Snacks cheese dip + 1 tablespoon of water and knead mixture until a thick, doughy paste forms. Shape into thumb-sized balls. Microwave gnocchi balls for 15 seconds. Keep warm. Combine ketchup + 1 teaspoon of water. Microwave ketchup solution for 15 seconds and drizzle over gnocchi. Serve immediately.

terrine normande

INGREDIENTS

1 serving Cheez-Its
1 bag Utz Onion Garlic Chips
1 bag pork rinds
1 packet ketchup

Smash Cheez-Its, Utz Onion Garlic Chips, and pork rinds separately. (We suggest Low-Fat Cheez-Its. This is the one gesture to health in this entire book.) Layer Cheez-It powder with Utz Onion Garlic Chip powder and top with pork rind mash in a small shot glass. Repeat. Top with 1 tablespoon of water. Microwave for 25 seconds. Remove from microwave and let cool. Invert to demold. Serve with a ketchup garnish for color.

+ +

←

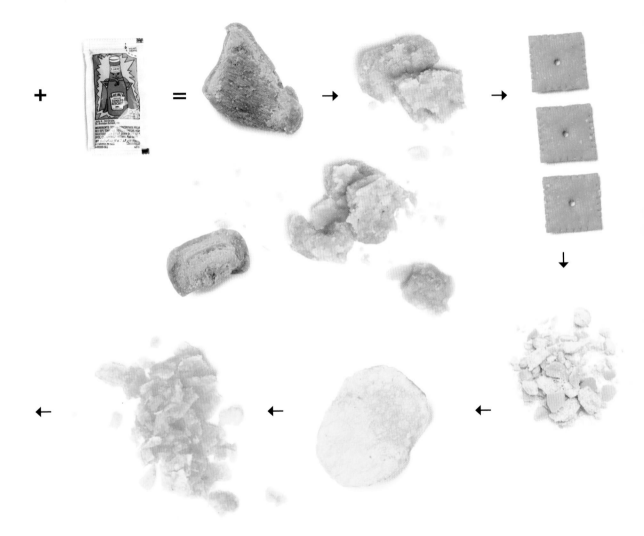

roti de porc algerien avec fruits garnis

INGREDIENTS

2 pork rinds
4 Hot Tamales
1 package Mixed Fruit Snacks
3 packets ketchup

Select two substantial pork rinds from bag and put to side. Finely chop Hot Tamales into bite-sized pieces. Combine Mixed Fruit Snacks with three packets of ketchup and Hot Tamale bits. Microwave for 15 seconds. Pour over pork rinds. Eat immediately.

cheddar feuilleté with green apple relish

INGREDIENTS

1 Twinkie
1 bag Cheetos
4 Green Apple Jelly Bellies

Deconstruct a Twinkie or use reserved cake from Triple Berry Compote Parfait recipe, and reconstitute into doughy texture. Roll out into a thin layer. Cut 3 small rectangles of the same size out of the dough. Pulverize a handful of Cheetos into a fine powder. Place Cheetos dust on top of each Twinkie dough rectangle. Chop Green Apple Jelly Bellies into tiny chunks and sprinkle on top of Cheetos powder. Layer rectangles on top of each other. Serve at room temperature.

white pizza with potatoes and anise caviar

INGREDIENTS

1 pack Keebler Crackers and Cheese
4 Licorice Jelly Bellies
1 bag Utz Onion and Garlic Chips

Separate Keebler Crackers and Cheese and place face up. Chop Licorice Jelly Bellies into small bits. Crumble Utz Onion and Garlic Chips and place on top of crackers. Microwave for 30 seconds. Top with Licorice bits. Eat while hot.

chilean frito corn chowder

INGREDIENTS

1 bag Fritos
1 bag Utz Red Hot Potato Chips
1 bag Utz Onion and Garlic Chips
3 Buttered Popcorn Jelly Bellies
4 packets ketchup
2 tablespoons water

Crush Fritos, Utz Red Hot Potato Chips, and Utz Onion and Garlic chips into chunky powder. Combine. Add 3 Buttered Popcorn Jelly Bellies. Add 4 packets of ketchup and 2 tablespoons of water. Microwave for 40 seconds. Mix well and serve with additional Fritos for dipping.

three cheese chilequiles

INGREDIENTS

1 pack Keebler Cheese and Crackers
1 pack Cheetos
5 packets ketchup
1 package Nacho Cheese Doritos
1 small can V8

Open Keebler Cheese and Crackers and place cheese-filling side up. Crush Cheetos using smash technique. Combine 5 packets ketchup with handful of Cheetos powder. Mix well. Let sit. Cover crackers with a layer of Doritos. Spread ketchup–cheese puff mixture evenly over the Doritos. Pour V8 over the entire plate. Microwave on high for approximately 1 minute. Remove from microwave. Top with remaining Cheetos powder. Serve.

 +  +  +

 +  =

les desserts

Lil' bites that will leave 'em wanting more ....

mocha nougat fondant

INGREDIENTS

Chocolate layers from 1 Mounds bar
1 packet Nescafé instant coffee
1 packet instant hot chocolate mix
1 Snickers bar (or 2 mini Snickers bars)

Deconstruct a Mounds bar and combine chocolate layers (can also use leftover layers from Tom Khaa recipe) with Nescafé and hot chocolate mix. Add hot water until a thickish paste forms. Cut Snickers bar(s) into even slices. Dip slices into chocolate paste. Plate in an interesting way. Cover with remaining hot chocolate mix.

twinkie napoleon

1 Twinkie
1 pack potato chips

Cut open Twinkie and remove inside cream filling. Reserve. Knead each Twinkie cake slice until it forms a doughy ball. Divide into 2. Roll out one dough ball into a thin layer. Crush all but a few potato chips into fine powder. Cover first Twinkie dough layer with a fine layer of crushed potato chips. Repeat and layer on top of each other to form a layer cake until Twinkie dough runs out. Cut layers into 2 even rectangular pieces. Take reserved Twinkie cream and cover one side with a thin layer of cream. Top with other cut side so a layered cake is formed. Cover with remaining cream. Top with whole potato chip. Serve immediately.

 +

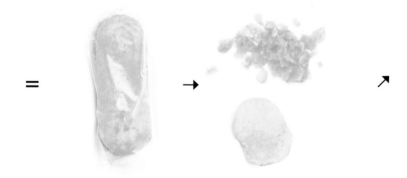

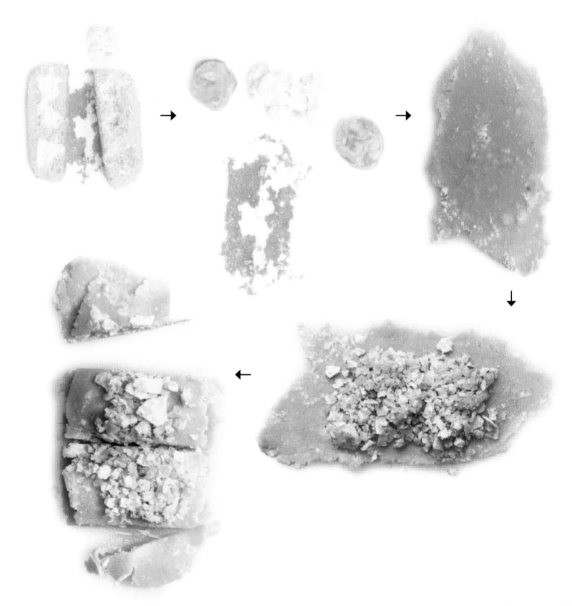

truffled berry praline purses

INGREDIENTS

2 Reese's Peanut Butter Cups
1 pack Potato Chips
1 Fruit Roll-Up

Remove Reese's Peanut Butter Cups from packaging and knead into balls. Crush potato chips into fine powder. Unroll Fruit Roll-Up and cut in half. Place one Reese's ball in center of one half Fruit Roll-Up. Sprinkle small amount of potato chip powder on top of Reese's ball. Fold up corners of Fruit Roll-Up to meet in center and form dumpling shape. Repeat as necessary. Enjoy.

=  +

INGREDIENTS *moelleux au chocolat*

1 chocolate cupcake
3 Hershey's Kisses

Slice chocolate cupcake in half horizontally. Remove cream from center, leaving two craters in the cake. Microwave 3 Hershey's Kisses for 30 seconds until melted. Stir to make into a paste. Fill craters with melted Kisses. Put cupcake back together. Microwave for 30 seconds or until starts to bubble. Serve immediately.

ho ho buche de noël

INGREDIENTS

1 Ho Ho
2 Sour Puckerooms Gummies
1 Nescafé packet

Remove hard chocolate shell from Ho Ho, taking care to preserve the bottom half. Break the remainder of the shell into bark-shaped shards. Place Puckerooms on top of the now deshelled Ho Ho. Decorate with bark-shaped shards. Place entire dessert into the reserved half of chocolate shell. Dust with Nescafé powder. Best served at room temperature.

banana praline paris brest

INGREDIENTS

1 Hostess Powdered Donette
4 Nutter Butters
1 Banana Twins (cream filling)
3 Toasted Marshmallow Jelly Bellies

Cut Powdered Donette in half. Open Nutter Butter and scrape peanut butter filling out. Reserve. Separate Banana Twins and remove cream filling. Combine banana cream filling and peanut butter to form a thick paste. Spread on one half of Powdered Donette. Chop (or cut) 3 Toasted Marshmallow Jelly Bellies into small relish-sized pieces and sprinkle over cream filling. Place other half of Powdered Donette on top. Garnish with Toasted Marshmallow Jelly Belly.

very cherry berry jelly belly clafoutis

INGREDIENTS

1 Vanilla Snack Pack Pudding
5 Very Cherry Jelly Bellies
1 Blueberry Pie Crust

Using reserved fruit pie crust technique from Triple Berry Compote Parfait recipe, deconstruct 1 Blueberry Pie and reserve top crust and filling, leaving bottom crust empty. Combine Vanilla Snack Pack Pudding with 5 Very Cherry Jelly Bellies. Place mixture in empty bottom pie crust to eat up.

circus peanut mound-arons

2 Circus Peanuts
1 Mounds bar filling
1 packet Wonka Cherry Yum Diddly Dip Fun Dip

Cut Circus Peanuts in half. Set aside. Carefully remove chocolate coating from Mounds bar and reserve. Combine coconut Mounds filling with ½ packet of Wonka Cherry Yum Diddly Dip. Mix until well incorporated and a pinkish paste has formed. Cover one half of Circus Peanut with Mounds mixture. Top with other half of peanut. Enjoy.

+

+

=

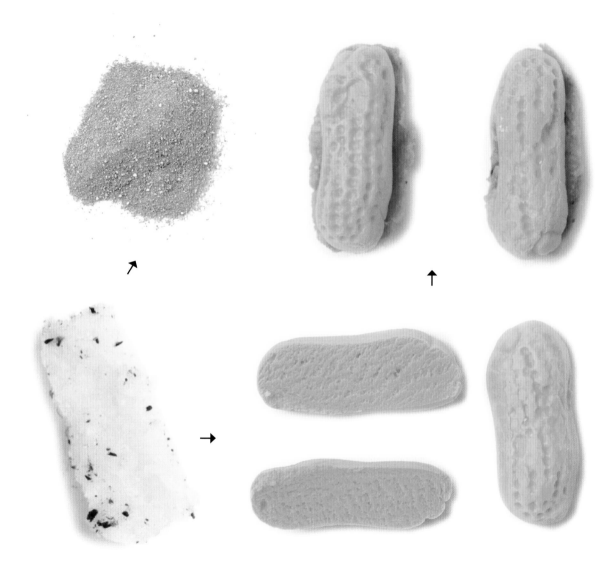

chocolate orange crème brulée

INGREDIENTS

1 Oreo
1 reserved Twinkie cream
1 pack orange Kool-Aid

Open Oreo and remove filling. Smash Oreo cookies into fine powder. Combine Oreo cream and Twinkie cream (see Triple Berry Compote Parfait recipe for cream technique). Place in small ramekin. Microwave for 20 seconds or until starts to bubble. Remove and dust top with orange Kool-Aid and Oreo cookie crumbles. Dig in.

croquembouche à l'americaine

INGREDIENTS

1 can 7Up (or other canned beverage)
6 Twinkies
1 jar Fluff
6 long Tootsie Rolls
12 Whoppers
1 small pack Jelly Bellies
1 pack Starlight Mint Candies
1 packet Wonka Razz Apple Magic Fun Dip

Wrap canned beverage in wax paper. Remove Twinkies from packaging and coat long sides of pastry cake in copious amounts of Fluff. Place Twinkies around paper-covered can, placing domed sides of Twinkies facing out, so that sides of Twinkies stick together, creating a ring-shaped cake around can. Place long Tootsie Rolls between Twinkies. Top Tootsie Rolls with 2 Whoppers each. Coat top of wax paper with more Fluff to create an even, thick glaze. Cover top portion of glazed wax paper with a mixture of Jelly Bellies. Place a handful of Starlight Mint Candies on top of can to creare a starburst shape. Top with a powdering of Wonka Razz Apple Magic Fun Dip. Dig in. Enjoy soda at the end. This makes a great wedding cake.

 +  +  +   +

 +  +  +

=   →  ↗

les amuses bouches

Mini morsels that pack a punch ....

cheddar-dusted popcorn

INGREDIENTS

1 bag Cheez Doodles
1 bag Wise Popcorn (butter flavor)
2 teaspoons water

Open bag of Cheez Doodles slightly along top to let air escape. Crumple bag with Cheez Doodles inside, until contents are reduced to a fine powder. Open popcorn bag. Add Cheez Doodles powder and two small spoonfuls of water. Close popcorn bag and shake vigorously to coat. Open. Enjoy.

 + +  +  =

INGREDIENTS *strawberry blinis*

1 Little Debbie Strawberry Shortcake Roll
1 bag Utz Salt 'n Vinegar Chips
1 Twizzler
Fluff for garnish

Cut Little Debbie Strawberry Shortcake Roll into slices. Pulverize a serving of Utz Salt 'n Vinegar Chips. Mash together slices of Strawberry Shortcake with Salt 'n Vinegar powder. This will yield a sticky mess at first. Continue kneading until a thick, pinkish paste forms. Form into small spheres. Microwave spheres for 30 seconds or until they fall into pancake shapes and brown slightly. Remove from microwave. Let cool. Top with chopped Twizzler relish and Fluff.

caramelized bbq balls

INGREDIENTS

1 bag Utz Bar-B-Q Potato Chips
2 Handi-Snacks Breadsticks 'n Cheez
1 tablespoon water
1 box Cracker Jacks

Pulverize a handful of Utz Bar-B-Q Potato Chips. Smash Handi-Snacks breadsticks into fine powder. Combine. Add 1 teaspoon water and mix until thick, doughy goo forms. Separate into small thumb-sized chunks and roll into sphere shapes. Using force, whack Cracker Jacks box to break down the popcorn into small chunks. Spill onto work surface and roll barbecue balls in Cracker Jacks pieces until coated. Enjoy.

INGREDIENTS

tartlette à l'onion

1 bag Utz Onion Rings
1 bag Onion Garlic chips
1 Handi-Snacks Crackers 'n Cheez

Select one well shaped Utz Onion Ring. Set aside. Choose one large, flat-ish chip and reserve. Smash a handful of Utz Onion Garlic chips and mix equal amounts of Handi-Snacks cheese dip with smashed chips. Place onion ring on top of reserved whole chip. Fill with cheese/chip mixture. Microwave for 10 seconds. Serve with natural garnish of choice.

INGREDIENTS

cheesestraws

1 small bag Cheetos
1 Handi-Snacks Breadsticks 'n Cheez

Using caution to not inhale while performing the smash, pulverize Cheetos into a fine powder. Open Handi-Snacks pack and coat breadsticks in cheese dip, leaving a small area at bottom uncoated. Roll coated breadsticks in Cheetos powder until well covered. Serve.

spicy sasparilla marinated pork bites

INGREDIENTS

1 bag pork rinds
1 small bottle root beer
Handful of Hot Tamales

Select several choice pork rinds. Pour a small serving of root beer in a microwave-safe bowl. Add 3 Hot Tamales/serving. Microwave for 3 minutes, removing mixture every minute to stir. Once Tamales have dissolved the mixture will take on a syrupy consistency. Let cool, then drizzle over pork rind. Garnish with chopped Hot Tamales and serve with chopsticks.

lebanese bird's nest bouchée

INGREDIENTS

1 Butterfinger Bite
1 serving potato sticks
1 teaspoon Fluff

Peel chocolate coating off of Butterfinger Bite. Reserve. Arrange potato sticks in a sunburst pattern. Top with teaspoon of Fluff. Place Butterfinger peanut center on top of Fluff. Garnish with a bit of extra Fluff and chocolate coating shaving. Serve.

INGREDIENTS

molé crunch

1 Oreo cookie
2 Hershey's Kisses
2 pork rinds

Separate Oreo and scrape out cream filling. Place filling and 2 Hershey's Kisses in heat-safe bowl. Microwave for 30 seconds. Remove and mix well to create a creamy texture. Crush Oreo cookie into powder. Dip one end of pork rind into Hershey/Oreo filling mixture. Top with Oreo cookie crumble. Eat with fingers for crunchy, sweet delight.

fromage fondant cube

INGREDIENTS

6 Cheez-Its
1 scoop Handi-Snack cheese dip
Buttered Popcorn Jelly Belly relish
2 slices Juicy Pear Jelly Belly

Select 6 nearly perfect Cheez-Its. Top 5 with globs of Handi-Snacks cheese dip, taking care to cover all the way to the edges. Once covered, assemble into a cube, leaving the sixth, uncoated Cheez-It to the side. Smash Cheetos into powder. Sprinkle a pinch of powder on top of each formed cube. Cut Buttered Popcorn Jelly Belly into tiny chunks. Shave two think slices off of Juicy Pear Jelly Belly. Top with Jelly Belly relish and slices. Top with remaining Cheez-It if desired. Eat in one bite.

 +  +

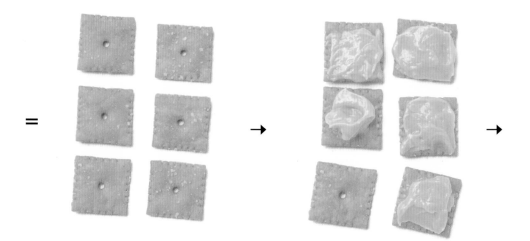

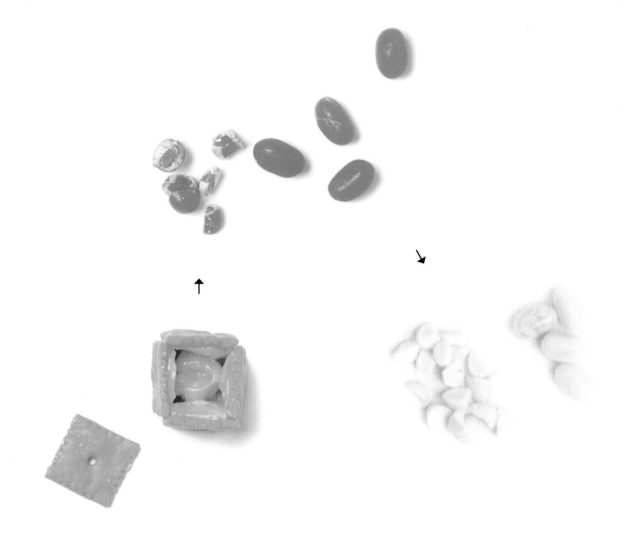

crunchy whole grain choco-pops

INGREDIENTS

1 bag Sun Chips
3 Tootsie Pops
Fluff for dipping

Pulverize Sun Chips into chunky bits. Pour on a clean surface. Unwrap Tootsie Pop of your choosing. Dip top half in Fluff. Coat in pulverized Sun Chips. Crunch and lick. (Or lick and crunch. Your choice.)

les cocktails

Liquid libations ....

INGREDIENTS **old-fashioned splash**

1 packet Wonka Cherry Yum Diddly Dip Fun Dip
1 Orange Kool-Aid packet
1 can 7Up
Cherry Dots

Mix equal parts of Cherry Yum Diddly Dip with Orange Kool-Aid.
Add to 7Up. Mix well. Float in Cherry Dots. Serve on ice.

= + +

INGREDIENTS **black russian twist**

1 small bottle Yoo-hoo
1 small bottle Coca-Cola
1 Twizzler

Mix Yoo-hoo with Coke. Stir in ice.
Serve with Twizzler straw.

+ =

INGREDIENTS

hi ho refresher

1 small bottle Fanta Orange
1 Laughin' Lemonade Kool-Aid Fun Fizz packet

Chill Fanta ahead of time in refrigerator. Pour Fanta in a tall glass when cool. Open Fun Fizz packet and drop into liquid. Serve immediately and watch the fizz fizz-out. Drink up!

= + +

wildberry taiwanese bubble tea spritzer

INGREDIENTS

1 bottle Nestea, lime flavor
1 can ginger ale
Welch's Berries 'n Cherries Fruit Snacks

Mix together Nestea, ginger ale, and Fruit Snacks. Let sit for 10 minutes. Add ice. Stir well. Drink.

sangria smasharita

INGREDIENTS

1 pack Wonka Razz Apple Magic Fun Dip
1 packet grape Kool Aid
1 can Coca-Cola
1 can grape soda
Handful Wonka Puckerooms

Combine 1 packet of Wonka Razz Apple Magic Fun Dip with 1 packet of grape Kool-Aid. Mix together Coke and grape soda. Add handful of Puckerooms and stir well. Dip rim of glass into Fun Dip/Kool-Aid powder. Fill with ice and pour in Coke/grape soda mixture. Sip and smile.

resources

Addicted? Here's where to stock up ....

Depending on your Junk Foodie addiction, here's a list of regional vendors, megastores, and big-time corporations that can feed your needs. We've left room at the end for you to fill in your local faces and begin building a personalized Junk Foodie lifestyle. With these guys, just remember to call first to confirm their stock. And never, ever, leave without buying more than your shopping cart can hold.

ALDI

www.aldi.us

The king of discount food retailers, Aldi boasts 1,000 stores in thirty-one states across the United States. Originally stocked with a small supply of select discounted products, Aldi began as a niche price-slashing store, but quickly grew to big-time success. It's the place to go for rock-bottom prices on junk food and although the selection may vary widely, for the budget-minded Junk Foodie, this is the place for "honest to goodness savings."

CALIFORNIA CHIPS

www.californiachips.com

If you wanna stay local, and you happen to be trapped in the land of eternal sunshine, give California Chips a call. The "official potato chip sponsor" of the LA Dodgers, this sporty snacker has an Earthquake chip that's sure to shake things up at your next Junk Foodie party.

CANDY BARON

www.thecandybaron.com

If you're strolling through San Francisco, take a trip down memory lane and hit the Candy Baron in Fisherman's Wharf. These guys'll tickle your nostalgia with treats like old school licorice and assorted gummies. (Yes! They have those Coca-Cola gummy bottles here!) You can't get gummy hot peppers anymore, but you can indulge your inner Junk Foodie a-plenty.

COSTCO

www.costco.com

Megastore to the max, you can't hide from these big boxes in the United States. Sure, they've got a great value goin' on, but more importantly, where else can you buy a super-sized portion of potato chips and a flat screen TV?

DYLAN'S CANDY BAR

www.dylanscandybar.com

Founded by Dylan Lauren, the daughter of Ralph Lauren, this eponymous store is the passion project of one sweet gal. Inspired by watching *Willy Wonka* when she was five years old, the Dylan empire has grown to sugar highs. The New York City store covers more than 15,000 feet, making it the largest candy store in the world! Boasting three floors of candy, alongside a soda fountain and an ice cream parlor, you can order goods online, but wouldn't you much rather go and drown in a sea of chocolate?

ECONOMY CANDY

www.economycandy.com

Known as the "Nosher's Paradise of the Lower East Side," aka the mecca of all things sugar-high, this little shop in Manhattan is the best of the junk. You can lose yourself on-site or order online.

HERSHEY'S CHOCOLATE WORLD

www.hersheys.com/chocolateworld

Okay. Pennsylvania just might be where it's at. Here's yet another Junk Foodie destination in the State of Sugar. Not only is this the home of all things candy, but you can also step it up and get an official Master's Degree in Chocolate Tasting. To top it off, they've also launched a "Create Your Own Candy Bar" program. So roll up your sleeves and plunge headfirst into this wonderland of junk. You can stock up on all things Hershey and hey, more chocolate just makes you a better person.

HOSTESS

www.hostesscakes.com

As the largest wholesale baker and distributor of fresh bakery products in the United States, Hostess Brands is the owner of all the deliciousness found in Hostess, Wonder Bread, Nature's Pride, Dolly Madison, Butternut Breads, and Drake products. Originally founded as Interstate Bakeries Corporation, it is the largest wholesale baker and distributor of fresh (well, as fresh as prepackaged cupcakes get) bakery goods in the States. Can you believe it was started by one guy named Ralph who started this empire selling bread loaves wrapped in gingham to grocery stores in Kansas City?

HYVEE

www.hy-vee.com

Should you be in the middle of the country, you can visit one of these employee-owned megastores and fill up on your dose of Junk Foodieness. Don't let their healthy-lookin' tagline fool you, there's plenty of junk in those center aisles, just steer clear of that shiny fruit-looking stuff and you'll be on your way to sugary success.

IT'SUGAR

www.itsugar.com

The rockstar of sugar rush, IT'sugar is more than a candy haven, it's a state of mind. With locations across the country and globe, these guys turn sugar into an experience. Get ready for irreverent, lickable fun when you step through these doors. It's the perfect place for a Junk Foodie to stock up and step it up.

KROGERS

www.kroger.com

The West Coast spot for super savings, give this big box a whirl next time you're out near the Pacific Ocean. They've always got an array of way-too-good-for-you nonsense stocked, but you can still do some serious Junk Foodie damage hidden in plain sight.

MARS

www.mars.com

You couldn't have Hershey's without Mars. Home of Snickers, Milky Ways, and M&M's, Mars, Inc., is the longtime competitor of the Pennsylvania candy giant. To this day operated as a family-owned business, Mars got its start from Frank C. Mars, whose mother taught him how to hand-dip candy. Famous for their secrecy, Mars is host to a variety of Junk Foodies faves. (We dare you to figure out how they put the M's on the M&M's....)

MCKEE FOODS

www.mckeefoods.com

These are the people that bring Little Debbie to life. Yup. You can't really go shopping there, but you might be able to make a pilgrimage and camp on the front lawn until they throw you a bone. Or a Banana Twin.

NOSTALGIC CANDY

www.nostalgiccandy.com

When Debbie and Mark Maley took their Wisconsin candy store online, little did they know they'd be fillin' more orders than their blood sugar could handle. This resource is great for getting everything from Big Hunk Bars (hubba hub) to Zero Bars (yeah, those are for real). Make sure to check out their Pez dispenser section. You can't really cook with 'em, but they sure do make for great Junk Foodie décor.

PATHMARK

www.pathmark.com

The discount food retailer of the East Coast, Pathmark is host to a variety of rare and unique Junk Foodiestuffs. We're particularly fond of the 24-hour locations for that late-night cookie crave.

PIGGLY WIGGLY

www.pigglywiggly.com

Is there any better name for one-stop Junk Foodie shopping? With more than 600 stores in seventeen states, Piggly Wiggly has been an American staple since 1916. Don't be scared by the larger-than-life Mr. Pig mascot. He won't bite. Just as long as you don't try to sauté him.

ROCKET FIZZ

www.rocketfizz.com

Purveyors of soda pop and candy cravings, this sweet shop is a Los Angeles staple. Offering more than 500 different bottled sodas from all corners of the country, Rocket Fizz will launch you into Junk Foodie heaven, candy bar in hand.

SAFEWAY

www.safeway.com

Boasting "Ingredients for Life," this big box is one way to feed your Junk Foodie lifestyle. Home to packaged goods galore, you can also stop for a tank of gas and petunias (select locations only).

SHOP RITE

www.shoprite.com

As one of the largest cooperatively owned discount retailers in the Northeast, this megastore is a particular favorite for its offering of uniquely oversized shopping carts. At least that's what they appeared to be for this author at 3 A.M. in Poughkeepsie during one random midnight visit. Not that late-night snack attacks would be a habit for you, dear reader.

SMOKY MOUNTAIN CANDY MAKERS

www.smokymountaincandymakers.com

This one might be a little too old-school to be super junk, but it's worth a trip if you find yourself in Tennessee. Made the old-fashioned way in a taffy machine from the 1940s, this family-owned business boasts flavors from Apple to Bubblegum. Plus, they've got a sugar-free selection just in case you, um, feel the need for a healthy alternative.

SUCKERS CANDY, INC

www.suckerscandyinc.com

You'd be a fool not to take this trip down memory lane if you pass through the Windy City. Filled to the brim with nostalgic sweet treats, Suckers fulfills all your retro needs. With treats like Flying Saucers and saltwater taffy, this is one Midwestern must-see!

SUPERVALU

www.supervalu.com

This is the guy to thank for getting you your Ding Dongs on time. As a supplier of more than 2,000 independent food retailers, the SUPERVALU fleet of trailer trucks helps stock grocery stores nationwide, from Jewel-Osco to Albertsons. Send 'em a thank you letter (and don't forget to include your favorite junk foodstuff—who knows, one of those trailers might show up at your house!).

TAQUITOS

www.taquitos.net

Not a taco shop, this online resource will give you the best and crunchiest of Junk Foodie snacks. They have a whole section devoted to chips and even a "Snacking Video" section for some really random facts to chew on. The "Snacking Stat" section will give you a great overview of what's hot and what's not, so get movin' and start learning! Remember, an educated Junk Foodie is a great Junk Foodie.

TASTYKAKE

www.tastykake.com

A Philadelphia original, this big-time bakery opened its doors in 1914 and hasn't stopped since. You can find a variety of Phillie-themed junk-food memorabilia on its website, or stalk the isles of Northeast grocers for a glimpse of Butterscotch Krimpets and Chocolate Juniors. Plus, their factory boasts an oven that's half the length of a football field.

TIM'S CHIPS

www.timschips.com

These are some wacky west coast flavors, folks. Made near the Cascade Mountains, these snacks are a Junk Foodie's dream. With potato chip flavors like Sweet Maui Onion and Luau Barbecue, Tim's fries up some exotic flavors that'll spice up any junky recipe.

UTZ

www.utzsnacks.com

Since 1921, when Bill and Salie Utz had a craving for a fresher potato chip, Utz has continually been pumpin' out potato crispiness. They've added some sweet and pretzely items over the years, but the crunchy starchy stuff still takes the cake for this Junk Foodie. You can order specialty items online, or see it live and in person by making the trek out to Hanover, Pennsylvania, for the Chip Trip tour through their 600,000 square foot facility.

WALMART

www.walmart.com

Founded by a Mr. Sam Walton, this superstore is one of the world's largest public corporations. And they've got the shopping carts to prove it. Go here to fill up on all the processed wonders you can imagine. But remember to bring protection. With deep discounts like these, it can get ugly in those aisles.

```
                  ST.
   ST# 2422 OP# 00002565 TE# 09 TR# 08102
   A H BKNG SD  003320001110 F
       12 AT  1 FOR   0.57
   SV AT 3OZ    007940002651         6.84 N
   SV 3OZ CB    007940002653         0.97 N
   SV ALOE 3Z   007940002652         0.97 N
   EMERY BD     007528074892         0.97 N
                    SUBTOTAL         1.12 N
   COUPON 79400 057940099276        10.87
   COUPON 79400 057940099276         1.00-0
   COUPON 79400 057940099276         1.00-0
   COUPON 74170 057417099276         1.00-0
   COUPON 33200 053320011033 F       1.00-0
   COUPON 33200 053320011033 F       1.00-0
   COUPON 33200 053320011033 F       1.00-0
   COUPON 33200 053320011033 F       1.00-0
   COUPON 33200 053320011033 F       1.00-0
   COUPON 33200 053320011033 F       1.00-0
                    SUBTOTAL         1.00-0
                       TOTAL         0.87
                  CASH  TEND         0.87
                  CHANGE DUE         1.00
                                     0.13

       # ITEMS SOLD 16

   TC# 2841 6624 6762 8927 8261

                    16
```

favorites

····································· use this space to jot down notes, tips,
tricks, and special stores for your junk